The Allegory

of the Cave

By Plato

(c. 380 bc.)

ISBN 978-1-452-80088-2

The Allegory of the Cave

Dialogue: Socrates and Plato's brother Glaucon

Socrates: And now let me show in a figure how far our nature is enlightened or unenlightened:—Behold! human beings living in a underground den, which has a mouth open towards the light and reaching all along the den; here they have been from their childhood, and have their legs and necks chained so that they cannot move, and can only see before them, being prevented by the chains from turning round their heads. Above and behind them a fire is blazing at a distance, and between the fire and the prisoners there is a raised way; and you will see, if you look, a low wall built along the way, like the screen which marionette players have in front of them, over which they show the puppets.

Glaucon: I see.

Socrates: And do you see men passing along the wall carrying all sorts of vessels, and statues and figures of animals made of wood and stone and various materials, which appear over the wall? Some of them are talking, others silent.

Glaucon: You have shown me a strange image, and they are strange prisoners.

Socrates: Like ourselves, and they see only their own shadows, or the shadows of one another, which the fire throws on the opposite wall of the cave?

Glaucon: True, how could they see anything but the shadows if they were never allowed to move their heads?

Socrates: And of the objects which are being carried in like manner they would only see the shadows?

Glaucon: Yes.

Socrates: And if they were able to converse with one another, would they not suppose that they were naming what was actually before them?

Glaucon: Very true.

Socrates: And suppose further that the prison had an echo which came from the other side, would they not be sure to fancy when one of the passers-by spoke that the voice which they heard came from the passing shadow?

Glaucon: No question.

situation of humans?

Socrates: To them the truth would be literally nothing but the shadows of the images.

Glaucon: That is certain.

Socrates: And now look again, and see what will naturally follow it' the prisoners are released and

2

disabused of their error. At first, when any of them is liberated and compelled suddenly to stand up and turn his neck round and walk and look towards the light, he will suffer sharp pains; the glare will distress him, and he will be unable to see the realities of which in his former state he had seen the shadows; and then conceive someone saying to him, that what he saw before was an illusion, but that now, when he is approaching nearer to being and his eye is turned towards more real existence, he has a clearer vision, what will be his reply? And you may further imagine that his instructor is pointing to the objects as they pass and requiring him to name them,—will he not be perplexed? Will he not fancy that the shadows which he formerly saw are truer than the objects which are now shown to him?

Glaucon: Far truer.

Socrates: And if he is compelled to look straight at the light, will he not have a pain in his eyes which will make him turn away to take and take in the objects of vision which he can see, and which he will conceive to be in reality clearer than the things which are now being shown to him?

Glaucon: True.

Socrates: And suppose once more, that he is reluctantly dragged up a steep and rugged ascent, and held fast until he's forced into the presence of the sun himself, is he not likely to be pained and irritated? When he approaches the light his eyes will be dazzled, and he will not be able to see anything at all of what are now called realities.

Glaucon: Not all in a moment.

Socrates: He will require to grow accustomed to the sight of the upper world. And first he will see the shadows best, next the reflections of men and other objects in the water, and then the objects themselves; then he will gaze upon the light of the moon and the stars and the spangled heaven; and he will see the sky and the stars by night better than the sun or the light of the sun by day?

gradually adapt

Glaucon: Certainly.

Socrates: Last of he will be able to see the sun, and not mere reflections of him in the water, but he will see him in his own proper place, and not in another; and he will contemplate him as he is.

Glaucon: Certainly.

Socrates: He will then proceed to argue that this is he who gives the season and the years, and is the guardian of all that is in the visible world, and in a certain way the cause of all things which he and his fellows have been accustomed to behold?

the sun

see then reason
Glaucon: Clearly, he would first see the sun and then reason about him.

Socrates: And when he remembered his old habitation, and the wisdom of the den and his fellow-

be glad of the change (margin note)

prisoners, do you not suppose that he would felicitate himself on the change, and pity them?

Glaucon: Certainly, he would.

Socrates: And if they were in the habit of conferring honors among themselves on those who were quickest to observe the passing shadows and to remark which of them went before, and which followed after, and which were together; and who were therefore best able to draw conclusions as to the future, do you think that he would care for such honors and glories, or envy the possessors of them? Would he not say with Homer, "Better to be the poor servant of a poor master", and to endure anything, rather than think as they do and live after their manner?

former life meaningless + depressing to him (margin note)

Glaucon: Yes, I think that he would rather suffer anything than entertain these false notions and live in this miserable manner.

old perspective is dark, impossible to see (margin note)

Socrates: Imagine once more such a one coming suddenly out of the sun to be replaced in his old situation; would he not be certain to have his eyes full of darkness?

Glaucon: To be sure.

Socrates: And if there were a contest, and he had to compete in measuring the shadows with the prisoners who had never moved out of the den, while his sight was still weak, and before his eyes had become steady (and the time which would be needed to acquire this new habit of sight might be very considerable) would

5

he not be ridiculous? Men would say of him that up he went and down he came without his eyes; and that it was better not even to think of ascending; and if any one tried to loose another and lead him up to the light, let them only catch the offender, and they would put him to death.

Glaucon: No question.

Socrates: This entire allegory you may now append, dear Glaucon, to the previous argument; the prison-house is the world of sight, the light of the fire is the sun, and you will not misapprehend me if you interpret the journey upwards to be the ascent of the soul into the intellectual world according to my poor belief, which, at your desire, I have expressed whether rightly or wrongly God knows. But, whether true or false, my opinion is that in the world of knowledge the idea of good appears last of all, and is seen only with an effort; and, when seen, is also inferred to be the universal author of all things beautiful and right, parent of light and of the lord of light in this visible world, and the immediate source of reason and truth in the intellectual; and that this is the power upon which he who would act rationally, either in public or private life must have his eye fixed.

Glaucon: I agree, as far as I am able to understand you.

Socrates: Moreover, you must not wonder that those who attain to this beatific vision are unwilling to descend to human affairs; for their souls are ever hastening into the upper world where they desire to

6

dwell; which desire of theirs is very natural, if our allegory may be trusted.

Glaucon: Yes, very natural.

Socrates: And is there anything surprising in one who passes from divine contemplations to the evil state of man, misbehaving himself in a ridiculous manner; if, while his eyes are blinking and before he has become accustomed to the surrounding darkness, he is compelled to fight in courts of law, or in other places, about the images or the shadows of images of justice, and is endeavoring to meet the conceptions of those who have never yet seen absolute justice?

b/c compelled (image) defend justice or justice used when world of light

Glaucon: Anything but surprising, he replied.

Socrates: Anyone who has common sense will remember that the bewilderments of the eyes are of two kinds, and arise from two causes, either from coming out of the light or from going into the light, which is true of the mind's eye, quite as much as of the bodily eye; and he who remembers this when he sees any one whose vision is perplexed and weak, will not be too ready to laugh; he will first ask whether that soul of man has come out of the brighter light, and is unable to see because unaccustomed to the dark, or having turned from darkness to the day is dazzled by excess of light. And he will count the one happy in his condition and state of being, and he will pity the other; or, if he have a mind to laugh at the soul which comes from below into the light, there will be more reason in this than in the laugh which greets him who returns from above out of the light into the den.

confusion when passing in or out of enlightened state

7

Glaucon: That is a very just distinction.

Socrates: But then, if I am right, certain professors of education must be wrong when they say that they can put a knowledge into the soul which was not there before, like sight into blind eyes.

Glaucon: They undoubtedly say this.

Socrates: Whereas, our argument shows that the power and capacity of learning exists in the soul already; and that just as the eye was unable to turn from darkness to light without the whole body, so too the instrument of knowledge can only by the movement of the whole soul be turned from the world of becoming into that of being, and learn by degrees to endure the sight of being, and of the brightest and best of being, or in other words, of the good.

Glaucon: Very true.

Socrates: And must there not be some art which will effect conversion in the easiest and quickest manner; not implanting the faculty of sight, for that exists already, but has been turned in the wrong direction, and is looking away from the truth?

Glaucon: Yes, such an art may be presumed.

Socrates: And whereas the other so-called virtues of the soul seem to be akin to bodily qualities, for even when they are not originally innate they can be implanted later by habit and exercise, the of wisdom more than anything else contains a divine element

8

which always remains, and by this conversion is rendered useful and profitable; or, on the other hand, hurtful and useless. Did you never observe the narrow intelligence flashing from the keen eye of a clever rogue—how eager he is, how clearly his paltry soul sees the way to his end; he is the reverse of blind, but his keen eyesight is forced into the service of evil, and he is mischievous in proportion to his cleverness.

Glaucon: Very true.

Socrates: But what if there had been a circumcision of such natures in the days of their youth; and they had been severed from those sensual pleasures, such as eating and drinking, which, like leaden weights, were attached to them at their birth, and which drag them down and turn the vision of their souls upon the things that are below—if, I say, they had been released from these impediments and turned in the opposite direction, the very same faculty in them would have seen the truth as keenly as they see what their eyes are turned to now.

Glaucon: Very likely.

Socrates: Yes, and there is another thing which is likely, or rather a necessary inference from what has preceded, that neither the uneducated and uninformed of the truth, nor yet those who never make an end of their education, will be able ministers of State; not the former, because they have no single aim of duty which is the rule of all their actions, private as well as public; nor the latter, because they will not

9

act at all except upon compulsion, fancying that they are already dwelling apart in the islands of the blest.

Glaucon: Very true.

Socrates: Then the business of us who are the founders of the State will be to compel the best minds to attain that knowledge which we have already shown to be the greatest of all-they must continue to ascend until they arrive at the good; but when they have ascended and seen enough we must not allow them to do as they do now.

Glaucon: What do you mean?

must come back down after ascending

Socrates: I mean that they remain in the upper world: but this must not be allowed; they must be made to descend again among the prisoners in the den, and partake of their labors and honors, whether they are worth having or not.

unfair?

Glaucon: But is not this unjust? Ought we to give them a worse life, when they might have a better?

Socrates: You have again forgotten, my friend, the intention of the legislator, who did not aim at making any one class in the State happy above the rest; the happiness was to be in the whole State, and he held the citizens together by persuasion and necessity, making them benefactors of the State, and therefore benefactors of one another; to this end he created them, not to please themselves, but to be his instruments in binding up the State.

Glaucon: True, I had forgotten.

Socrates: Observe, Glaucon, that there will be no injustice in compelling our philosophers to have a care and providence of others; we shall explain to them that in other States, men of their class are not obliged to share in the toils of politics: and this is reasonable, for they grow up at their own sweet will, and the government would rather not have them. Being self-taught, they cannot be expected to show any gratitude for a culture which they have never received. But we have brought you into the world to be rulers of the hive, kings of yourselves and of the other citizens, and have educated you far better and more perfectly than they have been educated, and you are better able to share in the double duty. Wherefore each of you, when his turn comes, must go down to the general underground abode, and get the habit of seeing in the dark. When you have acquired the habit, you will see ten thousand times better than the inhabitants of the den, and you will know what the several images are, and what they represent, because you have seen the beautiful and just and good in their truth. And thus our State which is also yours will be a reality, and not a dream only, and will be administered in a spirit unlike that of other States, in which men fight with one another about shadows only and are distracted in the struggle for power, which in their eyes is a great good. Whereas the truth is that the State in which the rulers are most reluctant to govern is always the best and most quietly governed, and the State in which they are most eager, the worst.

Glaucon: Quite true.

11

Socrates: And will our pupils, when they hear this, refuse to take their turn at the toils of State, when they are allowed to spend the greater part of their time with one another in the heavenly light?

Glaucon: Impossible, for they are just men, and the commands which we impose upon them are just; there can be no doubt that every one of them will take office as a stern necessity, and not after the fashion of our present rulers of State.

Socrates: Yes, my friend, and there lies the point. You must contrive for your future rulers another and a better life than that of a ruler, and then you may have a well-ordered State; for only in the State which offers this, will they rule who are truly rich, not in silver and gold, but in virtue and wisdom, which are the true blessings of life. Whereas if they go to the administration of public affairs, poor and hungering after the' own private advantage, thinking that hence they are to snatch the chief good, order there can never be; for they will be fighting about office, and the civil and domestic broils which thus arise will be the ruin of the rulers themselves and of the whole State.

Glaucon: Most true.

Socrates: And the only life which looks down upon the life of political ambition is that of true philosophy. Do you know of any other?

Glaucon: Indeed, I do not.

Socrates: And those who govern ought not to be lovers of the task? For, if they are, there will be rival lovers, and they will fight.

Glaucon: No question.

Socrates: Who then are those whom we shall compel to be guardians? Surely they will be the men who are wisest about affairs of State, and by whom the State is best administered, and who at the same time have other honors and another and a better life than that of politics?

qualities of rulers of State

Glaucon: They are the men, and I will choose them.

Socrates: And now shall we consider in what way such guardians will be produced, and how they are to be brought from darkness to light,—as some are said to have ascended from the world below to the gods?

how will they get true qualities?

Glaucon: By all means.

Socrates: The process is not the turning over of an oyster-shell, but the turning round of a soul passing from a day which is little better than night to the true day of being, that is, the ascent from below, which we affirm to be true philosophy?

Glaucon: Quite so.

Socrates: And should we not enquire what sort of knowledge has the power of effecting such a change?

Glaucon: Certainly.

Socrates: What sort of knowledge is there which would draw the soul from becoming to being? And another consideration has just occurred to me: You will remember that our young men are to be warrior athletes

Glaucon: Yes, that was said.

Socrates: Then this new kind of knowledge must have an additional quality?

Glaucon: What quality?

Socrates: Usefulness in war.

Glaucon: Yes, if possible.

Socrates: There were two parts in our former scheme of education, were there not?

Glaucon: Just so.

Socrates: There was gymnastic which presided over the growth and decay of the body, and may therefore be regarded as having to do with generation and corruption?

Glaucon: True.

Socrates: Then that is not the knowledge which we are seeking to discover?

Glaucon: No.

Socrates: But what do you say of music, which also entered to a certain extent into our former scheme?

Glaucon: Music, as you will remember, was the counterpart of gymnastic, and trained the guardians by the influences of habit, by harmony making them harmonious, by rhythm rhythmical, but not giving them science; and the words, whether fabulous or possibly true, had kindred elements of rhythm and harmony in them. But in music there was nothing which tended to that good which you are now seeking.

Socrates: You are most accurate in your recollection; in music there certainly was nothing of the kind. But what branch of knowledge is there, my dear Glaucon, which is of the desired nature; since all the useful arts were reckoned mean by us?

Glaucon: Undoubtedly; and yet if music and gymnastic are excluded, and the arts are also excluded, what remains?

Socrates: Well, there may be nothing left of our special subjects; and then we shall have to take something which is not special, but of universal application.

Glaucon: What may that be?

Socrates: A something which all arts and sciences and intelligences use in common, and which everyone first has to learn among the elements of education.

Glaucon: What is that?

15

b/c is math in all things

Socrates: The little matter of distinguishing one, two, and three—in a word, number and calculation:—do not all arts and sciences necessarily partake of them?

Glaucon: Yes.

Socrates: Then the art of war partakes of them?

Glaucon: To the sure.

war

Socrates: Then Palamedes, whenever he appears in tragedy, proves Agamemnon ridiculously unfit to be a general. Did you never remark how he declares that he had invented number, and had numbered the ships and set in array the ranks of the army at Troy; which implies that they had never been numbered before, and Agamemnon must be supposed literally to have been incapable of counting his own feet—how could he if he was ignorant of number? And if that is true, what sort of general must he have been?

Glaucon: I should say a very strange one, if this was as you say.

Socrates: Can we deny that a warrior should have a knowledge of arithmetic?

Glaucon: Certainly he should, if he is to have the smallest understanding of military tactics, or indeed, I should rather say, if he is to be a man at all.

Socrates: I should like to know whether you have the same notion which I have of this study?

Glaucon: What is your notion?

Socrates: It appears to me to be a study of the kind which we are seeking, and which leads naturally to reflection, but never to have been rightly used; for the true use of it is simply to draw the soul towards being.

Glaucon: Will you explain your meaning?

Socrates: I will try, and I wish you would share the enquiry with me, and say 'yes' or 'no' when I attempt to distinguish in my own mind what branches of knowledge have this attracting power, in order that we may have clearer proof that arithmetic is, as I suspect, one of them.

Glaucon: Explain.

Socrates: I mean to say that objects of sense are of two kinds; some of them do not invite thought(1) because the sense is an adequate judge of them; while in the case of other objects sense is so untrustworthy (2) that further enquiry is imperatively demanded.

Glaucon: You are clearly referring to the manner in which the senses are imposed upon by distance, and by painting in light and shade.

Socrates: No, that is not at all my meaning.

Glaucon: Then what is your meaning?

Socrates: When speaking of uninviting objects, I mean those which do not pass from one sensation to the opposite; inviting objects are those which do; in this latter case the sense coming upon the object, whether at a distance or near, gives no more vivid idea of anything in particular than of its opposite. An illustration will make my meaning clearer:—here are three fingers—a little finger, a second finger, and a middle finger.

Glaucon: Very good.

Socrates: You may suppose that they are seen quite close: And here comes the point.

Glaucon: What is it?

Socrates: Each of them equally appears a finger, whether seen in the middle or at the extremity, whether white or black, or thick or thin—it makes no difference; a finger is a finger all the same. In these cases a man is not compelled to ask of thought the question, what is a finger? for the sight never intimates to the mind that a finger is other than a finger.

perception

Glaucon: True.

Socrates: And therefore, as we might expect, there is nothing here which invites or excites intelligence.

Glaucon: There is not.

Socrates: But is this equally true of the greatness and smallness of the fingers? Can sight adequately perceive them? and is no difference made by the circumstance that one of the fingers is in the middle and another at the extremity? And in like manner does the touch adequately perceive the qualities of thickness or thinness, or softness or hardness? And so of the other senses; do they give perfect intimations of such matters? Is not their mode of operation on this wise— the sense which is concerned with the quality of hardness is necessarily concerned also with the quality of softness, and only intimates to the soul that the same thing is felt to be both hard and soft?

higher thinking

Glaucon: You are quite right.

Socrates: And must not the soul be perplexed at this intimation which the sense gives of a hard which is also soft? What, again, is the meaning of light and heavy, if that which is light is also heavy, and that which is heavy, light?

Glaucon: Yes, these intimations which the soul receives are very curious and require to be explained.

requires math

Socrates: Yes, and in these perplexities the soul naturally summons to her aid calculation and intelligence, that she may see whether the several objects announced to her are one or two.

Glaucon: True.

Socrates: And if they turn out to be two, is not each of them one and different?

Glaucon: Certainly.

Socrates: And if each is one, and both are two, she will conceive the two as in a state of division, for if there were undivided they could only be conceived of as one?

Glaucon: True.

Socrates: The eye certainly did see both small and great, but only in a confused manner; they were not distinguished.

Glaucon: Yes.

Socrates: Whereas the thinking mind, intending to light up the chaos, was compelled to reverse the process, and look at small and great as separate and not confused.

Glaucon: Very true.

Socrates: Was not this the beginning of the enquiry 'What is great?' and 'What is small?'

Glaucon: Exactly so.

Socrates: And thus arose the distinction of the visible and the intelligible.

Glaucon: Most true.

Socrates: This was what I meant when I spoke of impressions which invited the intellect, or the reverse—those which are simultaneous with opposite impressions, invite thought; those which are not simultaneous do not.

Glaucon: I understand and agree with you.

Socrates: And to which class do unity and number belong?

Glaucon: I do not know.

Socrates: Think a little and you will see that what has preceded will supply the answer; for if simple unity could be adequately perceived by the sight or by any other sense, then, as we were saying in the case of the finger, there would be nothing to attract towards being; but when there is some contradiction always present, and one is the reverse of one and involves the conception of plurality, then thought begins to be aroused within us, and the soul perplexed and wanting to arrive at a decision asks 'What is absolute unity?' This is the way in which the study of the one has a power of drawing and converting the mind to the contemplation of true being.

Glaucon: And surely, this occurs notably in the case of one; for we see the same thing to be both one and infinite in multitude?

Socrates: Yes, and this being true of one must be equally true of all number?

Glaucon: Certainly.

Socrates: And all arithmetic and calculation have to do with number?

Glaucon: Yes.

Socrates: And they appear to lead the mind towards truth?

Glaucon: Yes, in a very remarkable manner.

Socrates: Then this is knowledge of the kind for which we are seeking, having a double use, military and philosophical; for the man of war must learn the art of number or he will not know how to array his troops, and the philosopher also, because he has to rise out of the sea of change and lay hold of true being, and therefore he must be an arithmetician.

Glaucon: That is true.

Socrates: And our guardian is both warrior and philosopher?

Glaucon: Certainly.

Socrates: Then this is a kind of knowledge which legislation may fitly prescribe; and we must Endeavour to persuade those who are prescribe to be the principal men of our State to go and learn arithmetic, not as amateurs, but they must carry on the study until they see the nature of numbers with the mind only; nor again, like merchants or retail-traders, with a view to buying or selling, but for the sake of their military use, and of the soul herself; and because this will be the easiest way for her to pass from becoming to truth and being.

Glaucon: That is excellent.

Socrates: Yes, and now having spoken of it, I must add how charming the science is! and in how many ways it conduces to our desired end, if pursued in the spirit of a philosopher, and not of a shopkeeper!

Glaucon: How do you mean?

Socrates: I mean, as I was saying, that arithmetic has a very great and elevating effect, compelling the soul to reason about abstract number, and rebelling against the introduction of visible or tangible objects into the argument. You know how steadily the masters of the art repel and ridicule anyone who attempts to divide absolute unity when he is calculating, and if you divide, they multiply, taking care that one shall continue one and not become lost in fractions.

Glaucon: That is very true.

Socrates: Now, suppose a person were to say to them: O my friends, what are these wonderful numbers about which you are reasoning, in which, as you say, there is a unity such as you demand, and each unit is equal, invariable, indivisible,—what would they answer?

Glaucon: They would answer, as I should conceive, that they were speaking of those numbers which can only be realized in thought.

Socrates: Then you see that this knowledge may be truly called necessary, necessitating as it clearly does the use of the pure intelligence in the attainment of pure truth?

Glaucon: Yes, that is a marked characteristic of it.

Socrates: And have you further observed, that those who have a natural talent for calculation are generally quick at every other kind of knowledge; and even the dull if they have had an arithmetical training, although they may derive no other advantage from it, always become much quicker than they would otherwise have been.

Glaucon: Very true.

Socrates: And indeed, you will not easily find a more difficult study, and not many as difficult.

Glaucon: You will not.

Socrates: And, for all these reasons, arithmetic is a kind of knowledge in which the best natures should be trained, and which must not be given up.

Glaucon: I agree.

Socrates: Let this then be made one of our subjects of education. And next, shall we enquire whether the kindred science also concerns us?

Glaucon: You mean geometry?

Socrates: Exactly so.

Glaucon: Clearly, we are concerned with that part of geometry which relates to war; for in pitching a camp, or taking up a position, or closing or extending the lines of an army, or any other military maneuver, whether in actual battle or on a march, it will make all the difference whether a general is or is not a geometrician.

Socrates: Yes, but for that purpose a very little of either geometry or calculation will be enough; the question relates rather to the greater and more advanced part of geometry—whether that tends in any degree to make more easy the vision of the idea of good; and thither, as I was saying, all things tend which compel the soul to turn her gaze towards that place, where is the full perfection of being, which she ought, by all means, to behold.

Glaucon: True.

Socrates: Then if geometry compels us to view being, it concerns us; if becoming only, it does not concern us?

Glaucon: Yes, that is what we assert.

Socrates: Yet anybody who has the least acquaintance with geometry will not deny that such a conception of the science is in flat contradiction to the ordinary language of geometricians.

Glaucon: How so?

Socrates: They have in view practice only, and are always speaking? in a narrow and ridiculous manner, of squaring and extending and applying and the like— they confuse the necessities of geometry with those of daily life; whereas knowledge is the real object of the whole science.

Glaucon: Certainly.

Socrates: Then must not a further admission be made?

Glaucon: What admission?

Socrates: That the knowledge at which geometry aims is knowledge of the eternal, and not of aught perishing and transient.

Glaucon: That may be readily allowed, and is true.

Socrates: Then, my noble friend, geometry will draw the soul towards truth, and create the spirit of philosophy, and raise up that which is now unhappily allowed to fall down.

Glaucon: Nothing will be more likely to have such an effect.

Socrates: Then nothing should be more sternly laid down than that the inhabitants of your fair city should by all means learn geometry. Moreover the science has indirect effects, which are not small.

Glaucon: Of what kind?

Socrates: There are the military advantages of which you spoke, I said; and in all departments of knowledge, as experience proves, anyone who has studied geometry is infinitely quicker of apprehension than one who has not.

Glaucon: Yes indeed, there is an infinite difference between them.

Socrates: Then shall we propose this as a second branch of knowledge which our youth will study? *geometry*

Glaucon: Let us do so.

Socrates: And suppose we make astronomy the third— what do you say?

Glaucon: I am strongly inclined to it. The observation of the seasons and of months and years is as essential to the general as it is to the farmer or sailor.

Socrates: I am amused at your fear of the world, which makes you guard against the appearance of insisting upon useless studies; and I quite admit the difficulty of believing that in every man there is an eye of the soul which, when by other pursuits lost and dimmed, is by these purified and re-illumined; and is more precious far than ten thousand bodily eyes, for by it alone is truth seen. Now there are two classes of persons: one *people* class of those who will agree with you and will take (1) your words as a revelation; another class to whom (2) they will be utterly unmeaning, and who will naturally deem them to be idle tales, for they see no sort of profit which is to be obtained from them. And therefore you had better decide at once with which of the two you are proposing to argue. You will very likely say with neither, and that your chief aim in carrying on the argument is your own improvement; at the same time you do not grudge to others any benefit which they may receive.

Glaucon: I think that I should prefer to carry on the argument mainly on my own behalf.

Socrates: Then take a step backward, for we have gone wrong in the order of the sciences.

Glaucon: What was the mistake?

Socrates: After plane geometry we proceeded at once to solids in revolution, instead of taking solids in themselves; whereas after the second dimension the third, which is concerned with cubes and dimensions of depth, ought to have followed.

Glaucon: That is true, Socrates; but so little seems to be known as yet about these subjects.

Socrates: Why, yes, and for two reasons:—in the first place, no government patronizes them; this leads to a want of energy in the pursuit of them, and they are difficult; in the second place, students cannot learn them unless they have a director. But then a director can hardly be found, and even if he could, as matters now stand, the students, who are very conceited, would not attend to him. That, however, would be otherwise if the whole State became the director of these studies and gave honor to them; then disciples would want to come, and there would be continuous and earnest search, and discoveries would be made; since even now, disregarded as they are by the world, and maimed of their fair proportions, and although none of their votaries can tell the use of them, still these studies force their way by their natural charm, and very likely, if they had the help of the State, they would someday emerge into light.

Glaucon: Yes, there is a remarkable charm in them. But I do not clearly understand the change in the order. First you began with a geometry of plane surfaces?

Socrates: Yes.

Glaucon: And you placed astronomy next, and then you made a step backward?

Socrates: Yes, and I have delayed you by my hurry; the ludicrous state of solid geometry, which, in natural order, should have followed, made me pass over this branch and go on to astronomy, or motion of solids.

Glaucon: True.

Socrates: Then assuming that the science now omitted would come into existence if encouraged by the State, let us go on to astronomy, which will be fourth.

Glaucon: The right order. And now, Socrates, as you rebuked the vulgar manner in which I praised astronomy before, my praise shall be given in your own spirit. For every one, as I think, must see that astronomy compels the soul to look upwards and leads us from this world to another.

Socrates: Everyone but myself. To everyone else this may be clear, but not to me.

Glaucon: And what then would you say?

Socrates: I should rather say that those who elevate astronomy into philosophy appear to me to make us look downwards and not upwards.

Glaucon: What do you mean?

Socrates: You have in your mind a truly sublime conception of our knowledge of the things above. And I dare say that if a person were to throw his head back and study the fretted ceiling, you would still think that his mind was the percipient, and not his eyes. And you are very likely right, and I may be a simpleton: but, in my opinion, that knowledge only which is of being and of the unseen can make the soul look upwards, and whether a man gapes at the heavens or blinks on the ground, seeking to learn some particular of sense, I would deny that he can learn, for nothing of that sort is matter of science; his soul is looking downwards, not upwards, whether his way to knowledge is by water or by land, whether he floats, or only lies on his back.

Glaucon: I acknowledge the justice of your rebuke. Still, I should like to ascertain how astronomy can be learned in any manner more conducive to that knowledge of which we are speaking?

Socrates: I will tell you. The starry heaven which we behold is wrought upon a visible ground, and therefore, although the fairest and most perfect of visible things, must necessarily be deemed inferior far to the true motions of absolute swiftness and absolute slowness, which are relative to each other, and carry with them that which is contained in them, in the true number and in every true figure. Now, these are to be apprehended by reason and intelligence, but not by sight.

Glaucon: True.

Socrates: The spangled heavens should be used as a pattern and with a view to that higher knowledge; their beauty is like the beauty of figures or pictures excellently wrought by the hand of Daedalus, or some other great artist, which we may chance to behold; any geometrician who saw them would appreciate the exquisiteness of their workmanship, but he would never dream of thinking that in them he could find the true equal or the true double, or the truth of any other proportion.

Glaucon: No, such an idea would be ridiculous.

Socrates: And will not a true astronomer have the same feeling when he looks at the movements of the stars? Will he not think that heaven and the things in heaven are framed by the Creator of them in the most perfect manner? But he will never imagine that the proportions of night and day, or of both to the month, or of the month to the year, or of the stars to these and to one another, and any other things that are material and visible can also be eternal and subject to no deviation—that would be absurd; and it is equally absurd to take so much pains in investigating their exact truth.

Glaucon: I quite agree, though I never thought of this before.

Socrates: Then, in astronomy, as in geometry, we should employ problems, and let the heavens alone if we would approach the subject in the right way and so make the natural gift of reason to be of any real use.

Glaucon: That is a work infinitely beyond our present astronomers.

Socrates: Yes, and there are many other things which must also have a similar extension given to them, if our legislation is to be of any value. But can you tell me of any other suitable study?

Glaucon: No, not without thinking.

Socrates: Motion has many forms, and not one only; two of them are obvious enough even to wits no better than ours; and there are others, as I imagine, which may be left to wiser persons.

Glaucon: But where are the two?

Socrates: There is a second which is the counterpart of the one already named.

Glaucon: And what may that be?

Socrates: The second would seem relatively to the ears to be what the first is to the eyes; for I conceive that as the eyes are designed to look up at the stars, so are the ears to hear harmonious motions; and these are sister sciences—as the Pythagoreans say, and we, Glaucon, agree with them?

Glaucon: Yes.

Socrates: But this is a laborious study, and therefore we had better go and learn of them; and they will tell us whether there are any other applications of these sciences. At the same time, we must not lose sight of our own higher object.

Glaucon: What is that?

Socrates: There is a perfection which all knowledge ought to reach, and which our pupils ought also to attain, and not to fall short of, as I was saying that they did in astronomy. For in the science of harmony, as you probably know, the same thing happens. The teachers of harmony compare the sounds and consonances which are heard only, and their labor, like that of the astronomers, is in vain.

Glaucon: Yes, by heaven! And 'tis as good as a play to hear them talking about their condensed notes, as they call them; they put their ears close alongside of the strings like persons catching a sound from their neighbor's wall—one set of them declaring that they distinguish an intermediate note and have found the least interval which should be the unit of measurement; the others insisting that the two sounds have passed into the same—either party setting their ears before their understanding.

Socrates: You mean those gentlemen who tease and torture the strings and rack them on the pegs of the instrument: might carry on the metaphor and speak after their manner of the blows which the plectrum gives, and make accusations against the strings, both of backwardness and forwardness to sound; but this would be tedious, and therefore I will only say that these are not the men, and that I am referring to the Pythagoreans, of whom I was just now proposing to enquire about harmony. For they too are in error, like the astronomers; they investigate the numbers of the harmonies which are heard, but they never attain to problems-that is to say, they never reach the natural harmonies of number, or reflect why some numbers are harmonious and others not.

Glaucon: That is a thing of more than mortal knowledge.

Socrates: A thing which I would rather call useful; that is, if sought after with a view to the beautiful and good; but if pursued in any other spirit, useless.

Glaucon: Very true.

Socrates: Now, when all these studies reach the point of inter-communion and connection with one another, and come to be considered in their mutual affinities, then, I think, but not till then, will the pursuit of them have a value for our objects; otherwise there is no profit in them.

Glaucon: I suspect so; but you are speaking, Socrates, of a vast work.

Socrates: What do you mean? The prelude or what? Do you not know that all this is but the prelude to the actual strain which we have to learn? For you surely would not regard the skilled mathematician as a dialectician?

Glaucon: Assuredly not. I have hardly ever known a mathematician who was capable of reasoning.

Socrates: But do you imagine that men who are unable to give and take a reason will have the knowledge which we require of them?

Glaucon: Neither can this be supposed.

Socrates: And so, Glaucon, we have at last arrived at the hymn of dialectic. This is that strain which is of the intellect only, but which the faculty of sight will → *sight is deceptive* nevertheless be found to imitate; for sight, as you may remember, was imagined by us after a while to behold the real animals and stars, and last of all the sun himself. And so with dialectic; when a person starts on the discovery of the absolute by the light of reason only, and without any assistance of sense, and perseveres until by pure intelligence he arrives at the perception of the absolute good, he at last finds himself at the end of the intellectual world, as in the case of sight at the end of the visible.

Glaucon: Exactly.

Socrates: Then this is the progress which you call dialectic?

Glaucon: True.

Socrates: But the release of the prisoners from chains, and their translation from the shadows to the images and to the light, and the ascent from the underground den to the sun, while in his presence they are vainly trying to look on animals and plants and the light of the sun, but are able to perceive even with their weak eyes the images in the water (which are divine), and are the shadows of true existence (not shadows of images cast by a light of fire, which compared with the sun is only an image)—this power of elevating the highest principle in the soul to the contemplation of that which is best in existence, with which we may compare the raising of that faculty which is the very light of the body to the sight of that which is brightest in the material and visible world—this power is given, as I was saying, by all that study and pursuit of the arts which has been described.

Glaucon: I agree in what you are saying which may be hard to believe, yet, from another point of view, is harder still to deny. This, however, is not a theme to be treated of in passing only, but will have to be discussed again and again. And so, whether our conclusion be true or false, let us assume all this, and proceed at once from the prelude or preamble to the chief strain, and describe that in like manner. Say, then, what is the nature and what are the divisions of dialectic, and what are the paths which lead thither; for these paths will also lead to our final rest?

36

Socrates: Dear Glaucon, you will not be able to follow me here, though I would do my best, and you should behold not an image only but the absolute truth, according to my notion. Whether what I told you would or would not have been a reality I cannot venture to say; but you would have seen something like reality; of that I am confident.

Glaucon: Doubtless.

Socrates: But I must also remind you, that the power of dialectic alone can reveal this, and only to one who is a disciple of the previous sciences.

Glaucon: Of that assertion you may be as confident as of the last.

Socrates: And assuredly no one will argue that there is any other method of comprehending by any regular process all true existence or of ascertaining what each thing is in its own nature; for the arts in general are concerned with the desires or opinions of men, or are cultivated with a view to production and construction, or for the preservation of such productions and constructions; and as to the mathematical sciences which, as we were saying, have some apprehension of true being—geometry and the like—they only dream about being, but never can they behold the waking reality so long as they leave the hypotheses which they use unexamined, and are unable to give an account of them. For when a man knows not his own first principle, and when the conclusion and intermediate steps are also constructed out of he knows not what, how can he imagine that such a fabric of convention can ever become science?

Glaucon: Impossible.

Socrates: Then dialectic, and dialectic alone, goes directly to the first principle and is the only science which does away with hypotheses in order to make her ground secure; the eye of the soul, which is literally buried in an outlandish slough, is by her gentle aid lifted upwards; and she uses as handmaids and helpers in the work of conversion, the sciences which we have been discussing. Custom terms them sciences, but they ought to have some other name, implying greater clearness than opinion and less clearness than science: and this, in our previous sketch, was called understanding. But why should we dispute about names when we have realities of such importance to consider?

Glaucon: Why indeed, when any name will do which expresses the thought of the mind with clearness?

Socrates: At any rate, we are satisfied, as before, to have four divisions; two for intellect and two for opinion, and to call the first division science, the second understanding, the third belief, and the fourth perception of shadows, opinion being concerned with becoming, and intellect with being; and so to make a proportion:— As being is to becoming, so is pure intellect to opinion. And as intellect is to opinion, so is science to belief, and understanding to the perception of shadows. But let us defer the further correlation and subdivision of the subjects of opinion and of intellect, for it will be a long enquiry, many times longer than this has been.

Glaucon: As far as I understand, I agree.

Socrates: And do you also agree in describing the dialectician as one who attains a conception of the essence of each thing? And he who does not possess and is therefore unable to impart this conception, in whatever degree he fails, may in that degree also be said to fail in intelligence? Will you admit so much?

Glaucon: Yes, how can I deny it?

Socrates: And you would say the same of the conception of the good? Until the person is able to abstract and define rationally the idea of good, and unless he can run the gauntlet of all objections, and is ready to disprove them, not by appeals to opinion, but to absolute truth, never faltering at any step of the argument—unless he can do all this, you would say that he knows neither the idea of good nor any other good; he apprehends only a shadow, if anything at all, which is given by opinion and not by science;—dreaming and slumbering in this life, before he is well awake here, he arrives at the world below, and has his final quietus.

Still in shadows

Glaucon: In all that I should most certainly agree with you.

Socrates: And surely you would not have the children of your ideal State, whom you are nurturing and educating—if the ideal ever becomes a reality—you would not allow the future rulers to be like posts, having no reason in them, and yet to be set in authority over the highest matters?

Glaucon: Certainly not.

Socrates: Then you will make a law that they shall have such an education as will enable them to attain the greatest skill in asking and answering questions?

Glaucon: Yes, you and I together will make it.

Socrates: Dialectic, then, as you will agree, is the coping-stone of the sciences, and is set over them; no other science can be placed higher—the nature of knowledge can no further go?

Glaucon: I agree.

Socrates: But to whom we are to assign these studies, and in what way they are to be assigned, are questions which remain to be considered?

Glaucon: Yes, clearly.

Socrates: You remember how the rulers were chosen before?

Glaucon: Certainly.

Socrates: The same natures must still be chosen, and the preference again given to the surest and the bravest, and, if possible, to the fairest; and, having noble and generous tempers, they should also have the natural gifts which will facilitate their education.

Glaucon: And what are these?

Socrates: Such gifts as keenness and ready powers of acquisition; for the mind more often faints from the severity of study than from the severity of gymnastics: the toil is more entirely the mind's own, and is not shared with the body.

Glaucon: Very true.

Socrates: Further, he of whom we are in search should have a good memory, and be an unwearied solid man who is a lover of labor in any line; or he will never be able to endure the great amount of bodily exercise and to go through all the intellectual discipline and study which we require of him.

Glaucon: Certainly, he must have natural gifts.

Socrates: The mistake at present is, that those who study philosophy have no vocation, and this, as I was before saying, is the reason why she has fallen into disrepute: her true sons should take her by the hand and not bastards.

Glaucon: What do you mean?

Socrates: In the first place, her votary should not have a lame or halting industry—I mean, that he should not be half industrious and half idle: as, for example, when a man is a lover of gymnastic and hunting, and all other bodily exercises, but a hater rather than a lover of the labor of learning or listening or enquiring. Or the occupation to which he devotes himself may be of an opposite kind, and he may have the other sort of lameness.

Glaucon: Certainly.

Socrates: And as to truth, is not a soul equally to be deemed halt and lame which hates voluntary falsehood and is extremely indignant at herself and others when they tell lies, but is patient of involuntary falsehood, and does not mind wallowing like a swinish beast in the mire of ignorance, and has no shame at being detected?

Glaucon: To be sure.

Socrates: And, again, in respect of temperance, courage, magnificence, and every other virtue, should we not carefully distinguish between the true son and the bastard? For where there is no discernment of such qualities States and individuals unconsciously err and the State makes a ruler, and the individual a friend, of one who, being defective in some part of virtue, is in a figure lame or a bastard.

Glaucon: That is very true.

Socrates: All these things, then, will have to be carefully considered by us; and if only those whom we introduce to this vast system of education and training are sound in body and mind, justice herself will have nothing to say against us, and we shall be the saviors of the constitution and of the State; but, if our pupils are men of another stamp, the reverse will happen, and we shall pour a still greater flood of ridicule on philosophy than she has to endure at present.

Glaucon: That would not be creditable.

Socrates: Certainly not. And yet perhaps, in thus turning jest into earnest I am equally ridiculous.

Glaucon: In what respect?

Socrates: I had forgotten, that we were not serious, and spoke with too much excitement. For when I saw philosophy so undeservedly trampled underfoot of men I could not help feeling a sort of indignation at the authors of her disgrace: and my anger made me too vehement.

Glaucon: Indeed! I was listening, and did not think so.

Socrates: But I, who am the speaker, felt that I was. And now let me remind you that, although in our former selection we chose old men, we must not do so in this. Solon was under a delusion when he said that a man when he grows old may learn many things—for he can no more learn much than he can run much; youth is the time for any extraordinary toil.

Glaucon: Of course.

Socrates: And, therefore, calculation and geometry and all the other elements of instruction, which are a preparation for dialectic, should be presented to the mind in childhood; not, however, under any notion of forcing our system of education.

Glaucon: Why not?

Socrates: Because a freeman ought not to be a slave in the acquisition of knowledge of any kind. Bodily exercise, when compulsory, does no harm to the body; but knowledge which is acquired under compulsion obtains no hold on the mind.

true → Knowledge can't be forced

Glaucon: Very true.

Socrates: Then, my good friend, do not use compulsion, but let early education be a sort of amusement; you will then be better able to find out the natural bent.

Glaucon: That is a very rational notion.

Socrates: Do you remember that the children, too, were to be taken to see the battle on horseback; and that if there were no danger they were to be brought close up and, like young hounds, have a taste of blood given them?

Glaucon: Yes, I remember.

Socrates: The same practice may be followed in all these things—labors, lessons, dangers—and he who is most at home in all of them ought to be enrolled in a select number.

Glaucon: At what age?

Socrates: At the age when the necessary gymnastics are over: the period whether of two or three years which passes in this sort of training is useless for any other purpose; for sleep and exercise are unpropitious to learning; and the trial of who is first in gymnastic exercises is one of the most important tests to which our youth are subjected.

Glaucon: Certainly.

Socrates: After that time those who are selected from the class of twenty years old will be promoted to higher honor, and the sciences which they learned without any order in their early education will now be brought together, and they will be able to see the natural relationship of them to one another and to true being.

Glaucon: Yes, that is the only kind of knowledge which takes lasting root.

Socrates: Yes, and the capacity for such knowledge is the great criterion of dialectical talent: the comprehensive mind is always the dialectical.

Glaucon: I agree with you.

Socrates: These are the points which you must consider; and those who have most of this comprehension, and who are more steadfast in their learning, and in their military and other appointed duties, when they have arrived at the age of thirty have to be chosen by you out of the select class, and elevated to higher honor; and you will have to prove

Choosing

them by the help of dialectic, in order to learn which of them is able to give up the use of sight and the other senses, and in company with truth to attain absolute being: And here, my friend, great caution is required.

Glaucon: Why great caution?

Socrates: Do you not remark how great is the evil which dialectic has introduced?

Glaucon: What evil?

Socrates: The students of the art are filled with lawlessness.

Glaucon: Quite true.

Socrates: Do you think that there is anything so very unnatural or inexcusable in their case? or will you make allowance for them?

Glaucon: In what way make allowance?

Socrates: I want you, by way of parallel, to imagine a supposititious son who is brought up in great wealth; he is one of a great and numerous family, and has many flatterers. When he grows up to manhood, he learns that his alleged are not his real parents; but who the real are he is unable to discover. Can you guess how he will be likely to behave towards his flatterers and his supposed parents, first of all during the period when he is ignorant of the false relation, and then again when he knows? Or shall I guess for you?

Glaucon: If you please.

Socrates: Then I should say, that while he is ignorant of the truth he will be likely to honor his father and his mother and his supposed relations more than the flatterers; he will be less inclined to neglect them when in need, or to do or say anything against them; and he will be less willing to disobey them in any important matter.

parents > flatterers

Glaucon: He will.

Socrates: But when he has made the discovery, I should imagine that he would diminish his honor and regard for them, and would become more devoted to the flatterers; their influence over him would greatly increase; he would now live after their ways, and openly associate with them, and, unless he were of an unusually good disposition, he would trouble himself no more about his supposed parents or other relations.

flatterers > parents

Glaucon: Well, all that is very probable. But how is the image applicable to the disciples of philosophy?

Socrates: In this way: you know that there are certain principles about justice and honor, which were taught us in childhood, and under their parental authority we have been brought up, obeying and honoring them.

Glaucon: That is true.

Socrates: There are also opposite maxims and habits of pleasure which flatter and attract the soul, but do not

47

influence those of us who have any sense of right, and they continue to obey and honor the maxims of their fathers.

Glaucon: True.

Socrates: Now, when a man is in this state, and the questioning spirit asks what is fair or honorable, and he answers as the legislator has taught him, and then arguments many and diverse refute his words, until he is driven into believing that nothing is honorable any more than dishonorable, or just and good any more than the reverse, and so of all the notions which he most valued, do you think that he will still honor and obey them as before?

Glaucon: Impossible.

Socrates: And when he ceases to think them honorable and natural as heretofore, and he fails to discover the true, can he be expected to pursue any life other than that which flatters his desires?

Glaucon: He cannot.

Socrates: And from being a keeper of the law he is converted into a breaker of it?

Glaucon: Unquestionably.

Socrates: Now all this is very natural in students of philosophy such as I have described, and also, as I was just now saying, most excusable.

Glaucon: Yes, and, I may add, pitiable.

Socrates: Therefore, that your feelings may not be moved to pity about our citizens who are now thirty years of age, every care must be taken in introducing them to dialectic.

Glaucon: Certainly.

Socrates: There is a danger lest they should taste the dear delight too early; for youngsters, as you may have observed, when they first get the taste in their mouths, argue for amusement, and are always contradicting and refuting others in imitation of those who refute them; like puppy-dogs, they rejoice in pulling and tearing at all who come near them.

can't teach it to them too early

Glaucon: Yes, there is nothing which they like better.

Socrates: And when they have made many conquests and received defeats at the hands of many, they violently and speedily get into a way of not believing anything which they believed before, and hence, not only they, but philosophy and all that relates to it is apt to have a bad name with the rest of the world.

Glaucon: Too true.

Socrates: But when a man begins to get older, he will no longer be guilty of such insanity; he will imitate the dialectician who is seeking for truth, and not the eristic, who is contradicting for the sake of amusement; and the greater moderation of his

49

character will increase instead of diminishing the honor of the pursuit.

Glaucon: Very true.

Socrates: And did we not make special provision for this, when we said that the disciples of philosophy were to be orderly and steadfast, not, as now, any chance aspirant or intruder?

Glaucon: Very true.

Socrates: Suppose the study of philosophy to take the place of gymnastics and to be continued diligently and earnestly and exclusively for twice the number of years which were passed in bodily exercise—will that be enough?

Glaucon: Would you say six or four years?

Socrates: Say five years. And at the end of the time they must be sent down again into the den and compelled to hold any military or other office which young men are qualified to hold: in this way they will get their experience of life, and there will be an opportunity of trying whether, when they are drawn all manner of ways by temptation, they will stand firm or flinch.

Glaucon: And how long is this stage of their lives to last?

Socrates: Fifteen years. And when they have reached fifty years of age, then let those who still survive and

A) 50 yrs old

50

have distinguished themselves in every action of their lives and in every branch of knowledge come at last to their consummation; the time has now arrived at which they must raise the eye of the soul to the universal light which lightens all things, and behold the absolute good; for that is the pattern according to which they are to order the State and the lives of individuals, and the remainder of their own lives also; making philosophy their chief pursuit, but, when their turn comes, toiling also at politics and ruling for the public good, not as though they were performing some heroic action, but simply as a matter of duty; and when they have brought up in each generation others like themselves and left them in their place to be governors of the State, then they will depart to the Islands of the Blest and dwell there; and the city will give them public memorials and sacrifices and honor them, if the Pythian oracle consent, as demi-gods, but if not, as in any case blessed and divine.

Glaucon: You are a sculptor, Socrates, and have made statues of our governors faultless in beauty.

Socrates: Yes, Glaucon, and of our governesses too; for you must not suppose that what I have been saying applies to men only and not to women as far as their natures can go.

Glaucon: There you are right, since we have made them to share in all things like the men.

Socrates: Well, you would agree (would you not?) that what has been said about the State and the government is not a mere dream, and although

51

difficult not impossible, but only possible in the way which has been supposed; that is to say, when the true philosopher kings are born in a State, one or more of them, despising the honors of this present world which they deem mean and worthless, esteeming above all things right and the honor that springs from right, and regarding justice as the greatest and most necessary of all things, whose ministers they are, and whose principles will be exalted by them when they set in order their own city?

Glaucon: How will they proceed?

Socrates: They will begin by sending out into the country all the inhabitants of the city who are more than ten years old, and will take possession of their children, who will be unaffected by the habits of their parents; these they will train in their own habits and laws, I mean in the laws which we have given them: and in this way the State and constitution of which we were speaking will soonest and most easily attain happiness, and the nation which has such a constitution will gain most.

Glaucon: Yes, that will be the best way. And I think, Socrates, that you have very well described how, if ever, such a constitution might come into being.

Socrates: Enough then of the perfect State, and of the man who bears its image—there is no difficulty in seeing how we shall describe him.

Glaucon: There is no difficulty and I agree with you in thinking that nothing more need be said.

Made in the USA
Lexington, KY
15 January 2014